# Jake Hates to Skate

Copyright © 2005 by Dorothy J. Dixon. Sub 25785-DIXO
Library of Congress:                    2004097563
ISBN:           Softcover               1-4134-6989-2
                Hardcover               1-4134-6990-6

Publisher: Learning Leaders Ltd.
Dover, Delaware 19904
Printed in USA
Summary: Jake struggles to learn to skate;
Grandpa helps him to learn
1. Inner city life 2. Family life
3. African-Americans 4. Stories in rhyme

To order additional copies of this book, contact:
Xlibris Corporation
1-888-795-4274
www.Xlibris.com
Orders@Xlibris.com

# Jake Hates to Skate

By: Dorothy Jean Dixon

Pictures By: Duane Gillogly

# In Memory
## Of
## Witney Holland Rose, M.D.
## 1968-2003

"Mend my mind with the right book at the right time."

Thanks to Quincy A. Lucas for
editing and proofing.

"Grandpa, I hate to Skate. On these in-line skates, I am not so great."

"But Jake, my boy you will be great, if you just take your time. Your skates' like mine, are all in a line. So, it will take some time.

We'll take this date for you to skate.
In time you'll find that you skate great.
Now you just take your time."

"But Grandpa, I want to skate like you. You skate so great."

"Well Jake my boy, do not get it twisted,
when I was a boy,
I couldn't skate that great.
You'll find with time that skating is great,
if you just skate and skate."

13

The more Jake skated, the better
he got. Then Jake skated more.
Jake skates on in-line skates just
like his Grandpa more and more.
Now Jake does not hate to skate.

Name:_____ Date:_____

# Jake Hates to Skate

**Fillies:**

"Grandpa, I _____ to skate. On these in-line _____, I am not so _____."
Your skates' like mine are all in a _____." "Now you

just_____your time." "I want to _____ like you." "You
skate so _____. "You'll find with time that _____
is great, if you just skate and _____. The more Jake
_____, the better he got. Then_____skated more.

**_Words to Use_**: skates hate great line skate great take
skating skated skate Jake

# Jake Hates to Skate: Fillies Answers

"Grandpa, I hate to skate. On these

in-line skates, I am not so great."

Your skates' like mine are all in a line." "Now you just take

your time." "I want to skate like you." "You skate so great.

"You'll find with time that skating is great, if you just

skate and skate. The more Jake skated, the better he

got. Then Jake skated more.

Name:_____Date:_____

# Jake Hates to Skate

## Unscramble The Sentences:

1. I to skate Grandpa hate.

_____.

2. these skates not On in-line I am so great.

_____.

3. Jake boy will great, But you my be your take time if just your.

_____.

4. I like to you Grandpa want skate.

_____.

5. skate so You great.

_____.

# Jake Hates to Skate:

# Unscramble Answers

1. Grandpa I hate to skate.

2. On these in-line skates, I am not so great.

3. But Jake my boy, you will be great if you just take

   your time.

4. Grandpa I want to skate like you.

5. You skate so great.

# Jake Hates to Skate

Write a thank-you note to Grandpa. Pretend you are Jake. Write a letter to your Grandpa. Thank him for taking the time to teach you to skate. Tell Grandpa how happy you are now that you can skate. Tell him thanks for taking all day to teach you to skate. Ask Grandpa if he will skate with you at the playground on next Saturday.
Be sure to use the right date and write your name at the end.

## Jake Hates to Skate

## Words That Rhyme:

1. skate          make
2. Jake           mine
3. line           hate

~~~~~~~~~~~~~~~~~~~~~~~

## Find My Mate:

1. Skate          *line*
2 Jake            *hate*
3. mine           *skate*
4. line           *Jake*
5. hate           *mine*

## *Jake Hates to Skate*

## Words That Rhyme: Answers

1. skate                make

2. Jake                 mine

3. line                 hate

~~~~~~~~~~~~~~~~~~~~~~~~~~~~~~~~~~~~~~~~~~~~

## Find My Mate: Answers

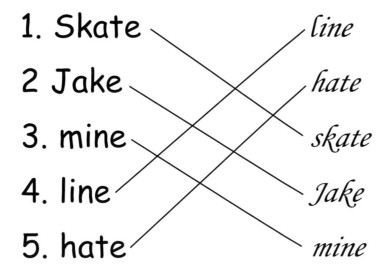

1. Skate               *line*

2 Jake                 *hate*

3. mine                *skate*

4. line                *Jake*

5. hate                *mine*

## *Jake Hates to Skate*
## Discovery Zone:

Discover the words and rewrite the sentences correctly.

1. Onthesein-lineskates,Iamnotsogreat.

_____

2. Intimeyou'llfindthatyouskategreat.

_____

3. Yourskateslikemineareallinaline.

_____

4. ThemoreJakeskated,thebetterhegot.

_____

5.WellJakemyboy,whenIwasaboy,Icouldn'tskatethatgreat.

_____

# Jake Hates to Skate

## Discovery Zone: Answers

Discover the words and rewrite the sentences correctly:

1. On these in-line skates, I am not so great.

2. In time you'll find that you skate great.

3. Your skates' like mine are all in a line.

4. The more Jake skated, the better he got.

5. Well Jake my boy, when I was a boy, I couldn't skate that great.

Name:_____ Date:_____

## Jake Hates to Skate

### Rewrite the sentences in print:

1. Jake hates to skate.

_____

2. On in-line skates, Jake is not so great.

_____

3. In time Jake found that skating was great.

_____

4. The more Jake skated, the better he got.

_____

5. Now Jake is great on in-line skates.

_____

# Jake Hates to Skate

## Rewrite the sentences in print: Answers

1. Jake hates to skate.

2. On in-line skates, Jake is not so great.

3. In time Jake found that skating was great.

4. The more Jake skated, the better he got.

5. Now Jake is great on in-line skates.

# Visits

Dorothy J. Dixon is a graduate of Johns Hopkins University with a Master of Science Degree in Reading Instruction. She has a long career in teaching reading. This author enjoys visiting schools, libraries, clubs, and other organizations to talk with students and adults about her books, and the techniques she uses to meet with success in developing reading skills for young people.

Invite Dorothy to visit your school, libraries or organization. Call her @ 302-677-0707 or email her at ddixon53@aol.com Re: school/library/organization visit

**Honorariums Welcomed**

# Upcoming Books:

Night Lights

Victoria's Quilt

Being First

Drenda is Lost

Marvelous Malcolm

Toria's Talented Twos

Serrick's Sensational Summer

# Mending Minds